Step by Step

The Story of Chocolate

It Starts with Cocoa Beans

Robin Nelson

Lerner Publications ◆ Minneapolis

Lerner Publications Company
An imprint of Lerner Publishing Group, Inc.
241 First Avenue North
Minneapolis, MN 55401 USA

For reading levels and more information, look up this title at www.lernerbooks.com.

Image credits: IMAGEMORE Co., Ltd./Getty Images, p. 3; 3000RISK/iStock/Getty Images, pp. 5, 23 (cocoa beans); aedkais/iStock/Getty Images, p. 7; renacal1/iStock/Getty Images, p. 9; Joá Souza/Brazil Photo Press/Getty Images, pp. 11, 23 (shipped); PATRICK KOVARIK/AFP/Getty Images, pp. 13, 23 (roasted); Boogich/iStock/Getty Images, p. 15; Deyan Georgiev/Shutterstock.com, p. 17; Olivier Polet/Corbis/Getty Images, p. 19; marka/Universal Images Group/Getty Images, pp. 21, 23 (wrapped); Martinan/iStock/Getty Images, p. 22.Cover: artisteer/iStock/Getty Images (chocolate); Pierre-Yves Babelon/Moment/Getty Images (beans).

Main body text set in Mikado a Medium.
Typeface provided by HVD Fonts.

Editor: Andrea Nelson
Lerner Team: Martha Kranes

Library of Congress Cataloging-in-Publication Data

Names: Nelson, Robin, 1971- author.
Title: The story of chocolate : it starts with cocoa beans / Robin Nelson.
Description: Minneapolis : Lerner Publications, 2021. | Series: Step by step | Includes bibliographical references and index. | Audience: Ages 4-8. | Audience: Grades K-1. | Summary: "How does a cocoa bean become a delicious chocolate bar? Find out through fun text and mouthwatering photos!"– Provided by publisher.
Identifiers: LCCN 2019035043 (print) | LCCN 2019035044 (ebook) | ISBN 9781541597273 (library binding) | ISBN 9781728401102 (ebook)
Subjects: LCSH: Chocolate—Juvenile literature. | Chocolate processing—Juvenile literature. | Cacao—Juvenile literature.
Classification: LCC TP640 .N45 2021 (print) | LCC TP640 (ebook) | DDC 663/.92—dc23

LC record available at https://lccn.loc.gov/2019035043
LC ebook record available at https://lccn.loc.gov/2019035044

Manufactured in the United States of America
1-47831-48271-11/21/2019

I love chocolate!

How is it made?

Cocoa beans grow.

Workers open
the pods.

The sun dries
the beans.

The beans are
shipped to a factory.

The beans are roasted.

Machines mash
the beans.

The chocolate
is mixed.

Next, chocolate is poured.

The chocolate is wrapped.

I eat my favorite treat!

Picture Glossary

cocoa beans

roasted

shipped

wrapped

Read More

Fretland VanVoorst, Jenny. *Chocolate: How Is It Made?* Minneapolis: Jump!, 2017.

Hansen, Grace. *How Is Chocolate Made?* Minneapolis: Abdo Kids, 2018.

Heos, Bridget. *From Cocoa Beans to Chocolate.* Mankato, MN: Amicus, 2018.

Index